Keto Machine Recipes

30 Easy, Healthy and Low-Carb Ketogenic Bread Machine Recipes for Baking Healthy Homemade Bread

By Marie Folher

Copyright Disclaimer

Disclaimer

Please note the information contained within this document is for educational and entertainment purposes only. Any of the information shouldn't be taken as medical advice. All effort has been executed to present accurate, up to date, and reliable, complete information. No warranties of any kind are declared or implied. Readers acknowledge that the author is not engaging in the rendering of legal, financial, medical or professional advice. The content within this book has been derived from various sources. Please consult a licensed professional before attempting any techniques outlined in this book.

By reading this document, the reader agrees that under no circumstances is the author responsible for any losses, direct or indirect, which are incurred as a result of the use of the information contained within this document, including, but not limited to, — errors, omissions, or inaccuracies.

Table of Contents

Introduction

To make our lives better, technology is coming up with new innovative machines every day. One such device that gives great quality results with little to no effort is a bread machine. As the name suggests, a bread machine is used to make homemade bread. It's convenient as it can be. You only need to put in the ingredients for the bread in the machine and wait. In a few hours, you can have the best fresh-baked bread first thing in the morning that suits your requirements. You can also just leave it through the night, and it will automatically switch off when the baking is completed. Its design makes it easy to carry around and place in the kitchen and puts fewer burdens on your pocket. It is becoming more and more popular as days pass by. One of the most important benefits you can get is that you can adjust the recipes of different loaves of bread according to your needs. Nowadays, people are following different types of diets, and this machine helps them in that endeavor.

Bread is a staple at every home, and it is hard to imagine a morning without it. During dieting, it is difficult to buy and make items and it's sometimes very costly. The bread machine helps you make the bread you want with ease.

One of the most popular forms of diet is the Keto diet, in which the person has to consume low amounts of carbohydrates and high amounts of fats. Some may say that bread is a fully carbohydrate-rich food that keto dieters should avoid, but there are many ways to make keto-friendly bread. Just by replacing high starchy flour with other types of flour like almond flour or sourdough, you can get low carb bread to eat, and all this can be made without any effort using the bread machine.

Savory Bread Recipes

Yeast Bread

Preparation time: 10 minutes

Cooking time: 4 hours

Total time: 4 hours and 10 minutes

Serving: 1 ½ pounds / 12 slices

Nutritional Info (Per Slice):

162 Cal | 11.3 g Fat | 8.1 g Protein | 7 g Carb | 2.8 g Fiber | 4 g Net Carb

Ingredients:

2 ¼ teaspoons dry yeast

1/2 teaspoon and 1 tablespoon erythritol sweetener, divided

1 1/8 cups warm water, at 100°F / 38°C

3 tablespoons avocado oil

1 cup / 100 grams almond flour

¼ cup / 35 grams oat flour

¾ cup / 100 grams soy flour

½ cup / 65 grams ground flax meal

1 1/2 teaspoons baking powder

1 teaspoon salt

Directions:

1.   Gather all the ingredients for the bread and plug in the bread machine having the capacity of 2 pounds of bread recipe.

2.   Pour water into the bread bucket, stir in ½ teaspoon sugar and yeast and let it rest for 10 minutes until emulsified.

3.   Meanwhile, take a large bowl, place the remaining ingredients in it and stir until mixed.

4.   Pour flour mixture over yeast mixture in the bread bucket, shut the lid, select the "basic/white" cycle or "low-carb" setting

and then press the up/down arrow button to adjust baking time according to your bread machine; it will take 3 to 4 hours.

5.   Then press the crust button to select light crust if available, and press the "start/stop" button to switch on the bread machine.

6.   When the bread machine beeps, open the lid, then take out the bread basket and lift out the bread.

7.   Let bread cool on a wire rack for 1 hour, then cut it into twelve slices and serve.

Cream Cheese Bread

Preparation time: 10 minutes

Cooking time: 4 hours

Total time: 4 hours and 10 minutes

Serving: 1 ½ pounds / 12 slices

Nutritional Info (Per Slice):

98 Cal | 7.9 g Fat | 3.5 g Protein | 2.6 g Carb | 0.4 g Fiber | 2.2 g Net Carb

Ingredients:

¼ cup / 60 grams butter, grass-fed, unsalted

1 cup and 3 tablespoons / 140 grams cream cheese, softened

4 egg yolks, pasteurized

1 teaspoon vanilla extract, unsweetened

1 teaspoon baking powder

¼ teaspoon of sea salt

2 tablespoons monk fruit powder

½ cup / 65 grams peanut flour

Directions:

1.   Gather all the ingredients for the bread and plug in the bread machine having the capacity of 2 pounds of bread recipe.

2.   Take a large bowl, place butter in it, beat in cream cheese until thoroughly combined and then beat in egg yolks, vanilla, baking powder, salt, and monk fruit powder until well combined.

3.   Add egg mixture into the bread bucket, top with flour, shut the lid, select the "basic/white" cycle or "low-carb" setting and then press the up/down arrow button to adjust baking time according to your bread machine; it will take 3 to 4 hours.

4.   Then press the crust button to select light crust if available, and press the "start/stop" button to switch on the bread machine.

5.   When the bread machine beeps, open the lid, then take out the bread basket and lift out the bread.

6.   Let bread cool on a wire rack for 1 hour, then cut it into twelve slices and serve.

Lemon Poppy Seed Bread

Preparation time: 10 minutes

Cooking time: 4 hours

Total time: 4 hours and 10 minutes

Serving: 1 pound / 6 slices

Nutritional Info (Per Slice):

201 Cal | 17.5 g Fat | 8.2 g Protein | 5.8 g Carb | 3 g Fiber | 2.8 g Net Carb

Ingredients:

3 eggs, pasteurized

1 ½ tablespoons butter, grass-fed, unsalted, melted

1 ½ tablespoons lemon juice

1 lemon, zested

1 ½ cups / 150 grams almond flour

¼ cup / 50 grams erythritol sweetener

¼ teaspoon baking powder

1 tablespoon poppy seeds

Directions:

1.   Gather all the ingredients for the bread and plug in the bread machine having the capacity of 1 pound of bread recipe.

2.   Take a large bowl, crack eggs in it and then beat in butter, lemon juice, and lemon zest until combined.

3.   Take a separate large bowl, add flour in it and then stir in sweetener, baking powder, and poppy seeds until mixed.

4.   Add egg mixture into the bread bucket, top with flour mixture, shut the lid, select the "basic/white" cycle or "low-carb" setting and then press the up/down arrow button to adjust baking time according to your bread machine; it will take 3 to 4 hours.

5. Then press the crust button to select light crust if available, and press the "start/stop" button to switch on the bread machine.

6. When the bread machine beeps, open the lid, then take out the bread basket and lift out the bread.

7. Let bread cool on a wire rack for 1 hour, then cut it into six slices and serve.

Almond Meal Bread

Preparation time: 10 minutes

Cooking time: 4 hours

Total time: 4 hours and 10 minutes

Serving: 1 ½ pounds / 10 slices

Nutritional Info (Per Slice):

104 Cal | 8.8 g Fat | 4 g Protein | 2.1 g Carb | 1.8 g Fiber | 0.3 g Net Carb

Ingredients:

4 eggs, pasteurized

¼ cup / 60 ml melted coconut oil

1 tablespoon apple cider vinegar

2 ¼ cups / 215 grams almond meal

1 teaspoon baking soda

¼ cup / 35 grams ground flaxseed meal

1 teaspoon onion powder

1 tablespoon minced garlic

1 teaspoon of sea salt

1 teaspoon chopped sage leaves

1 teaspoon fresh thyme

1 teaspoon chopped rosemary leaves

Directions:

1.   Gather all the ingredients for the bread and plug in the bread machine having the capacity of 2 pounds of bread recipe.

2.   Take a large bowl, crack eggs in it and then beat in coconut oil and vinegar until well blended.

3.   Take a separate large bowl, place the almond meal in it, add remaining ingredients, and stir until well mixed.

4.   Add egg mixture into the bread bucket, top with flour mixture, shut the lid, select the "basic/white" cycle or "low-carb" setting and then press the up/down arrow button to adjust baking time according to your bread machine; it will take 3 to 4 hours.

5.   Then press the crust button to select light crust if available, and press the "start/stop" button to switch on the bread machine.

6.   When the bread machine beeps, open the lid, then take out the bread basket and lift out the bread.

7.   Let bread cool on a wire rack for 1 hour, then cut it into ten slices and serve.

Macadamia Nut Bread

Preparation time: 10 minutes

Cooking time: 4 hours

Total time: 4 hours and 10 minutes

Serving: 1 pound / 8 slices

Nutritional Info (Per Slice):

155 Cal | 14.3 g Fat | 5.6 g Protein | 3.9 g Carb | 3 g Fiber | 0.9 g Net Carb

Ingredients:

1 cup / 135 grams macadamia nuts

5 eggs, pasteurized

½ teaspoon apple cider vinegar

¼ cup / 30 grams coconut flour

½ teaspoon baking soda

Directions:

1.   Gather all the ingredients for the bread and plug in the bread machine having the capacity of 1 pound of bread recipe.

2.   Place nuts in a blender, pulse for 2 to 3 minutes until mixture reaches a consistency of butter, and then blend in eggs and vinegar until smooth.

3.   Stir in flour and baking soda until well mixed.

4.   Add the batter into the bread bucket, shut the lid, select the "basic/white" cycle or "low-carb" setting and then press the up/down arrow button to adjust baking time according to your bread machine; it will take 3 to 4 hours.

5.   Then press the crust button to select light crust if available, and press the "start/stop" button to switch on the bread machine.

6.   When the bread machine beeps, open the lid, then take out the bread basket and lift out the bread.

7.   Let bread cool on a wire rack for 1 hour, then cut it into eight slices and serve.

Cauliflower and Garlic Bread

Preparation time: 10 minutes

Cooking time: 4 hours

Total time: 4 hours and 10 minutes

Serving: 1 ½ pounds / 9 slices

Nutritional Info (Per Slice):

108 Cal | 8 g Fat | 6 g Protein | 8 g Carb | 5 g Fiber | 3 g Net Carb

Ingredients:

5 eggs, pasteurized, separated

2/3 cup / 85 grams coconut flour

1 ½ cup / 300 grams riced cauliflower

1 teaspoon minced garlic

½ teaspoon of sea salt

½ tablespoon chopped rosemary

½ tablespoon chopped parsley

¾ tablespoon baking powder

3 tablespoons melted butter, grass-fed, unsalted

Directions:

1.   Gather all the ingredients for the bread and plug in the bread machine having the capacity of 2 pounds of bread recipe.

2.   Take a medium bowl, place cauliflower rice in it, cover with a plastic wrap, and then microwave for 3 to 4 minutes until steamed.

3.   Then drain the cauliflower, wrap in cheesecloth and twist well to squeeze out moisture as much as possible, set aside until required.

4.   Place egg whites in a large bowl and whisk by using an electric whisker until stiff peaks form.

5.   Then transfer one-fourth of whipped egg whites into a food processor, add remaining ingredients except for cauliflower and pulse for 2 minutes until blended.

6. Add cauliflower rice, pulse for 2 minutes until well combined, and then pulse in remaining egg whites until just mixed.

7. Add batter into the bread bucket, shut the lid, select the "basic/white" cycle or "low-carb" setting and then press the up/down arrow button to adjust baking time according to your bread machine; it will take 3 to 4 hours.

8. Then press the crust button to select light crust if available, and press the "start/stop" button to switch on the bread machine.

9. When the bread machine beeps, open the lid, then take out the bread basket and lift out the bread.

10. Let bread cool on a wire rack for 1 hour, then cut it into nine slices and serve.

Cheesy Garlic Bread

Preparation time: 10 minutes

Cooking time: 4 hours

Total time: 4 hours and 10 minutes

Serving: 2 pounds / 16 slices

Nutritional Info (Per Slice):

250 Cal | 14.5 g Fat | 7.2 g Protein | 3 g Carb | 1.6 g Fiber | 1.4 g
Net Carb

Ingredients:

For the Bread:

5 eggs, pasteurized

2 cups / 200 grams almond flour

1/2 teaspoon xanthan gum

1 teaspoon garlic powder

1 teaspoon salt

1 teaspoon parsley

1 teaspoon Italian seasoning

1 teaspoon dried oregano

1 stick of butter, grass-fed, unsalted, melted

1 cup / 100 grams grated mozzarella cheese

2 tablespoons ricotta cheese

1 cup / 235 grams grated cheddar cheese

1/3 cup / 30 grams grated parmesan cheese

For the Topping:

½ stick of butter, grass-fed, unsalted, melted

1 teaspoon garlic powder

Directions:

1.   Gather all the ingredients for the bread and plug in the bread machine having the capacity of 2 pounds of bread recipe.

2.   Take a large bowl, crack eggs in it and then whisk until blended.

3.   Take a separate large bowl, place flour in it, and stir in xanthan gum and all the cheeses until well combined.

4.   Take a medium bowl, place butter in it, add all the seasonings in it, and stir until mixed.

5.   Add egg mixture into the bread bucket, top with seasoning mixture and flour mixture, shut the lid, select the "basic/white" cycle or "low-carb" setting and then press the up/down arrow button to adjust baking time according to your bread machine; it will take 3 to 4 hours.

6.   Then press the crust button to select light crust if available, and press the "start/stop" button to switch on the bread machine.

7.   When the bread machine beeps, open the lid, then take out the bread basket and lift out the bread.

8.   Prepare the topping by mixing together melted butter and garlic powder and brush the mixture on top of the bread.

9.   Let bread cool on a wire rack for 1 hour, then cut it into sixteen slices and serve.

Rosemary Bread

Preparation time: 10 minutes

Cooking time: 4 hours

Total time: 4 hours and 10 minutes

Serving: 1 pound / 10 slices

Nutritional Info (Per Slice):

147 Cal | 12.5 g Fat | 4.6 g Protein | 3.5 g Carb | 2 g Fiber | 1.5 g Net Carb

Ingredients:

6 eggs, pasteurized

8 tablespoons butter, grass-fed, unsalted, melted

½ cup /65 grams coconut flour

1 teaspoon baking powder

1/4 teaspoon salt

1/2 teaspoon onion powder

1 teaspoon garlic powder

2 teaspoons dried rosemary

Directions:

1. Gather all the ingredients for the bread and plug in the bread machine having the capacity of 1 pound of bread recipe.

2. Take a large bowl, crack eggs in it, and then slowly beat in the melted butter until well combined.

3. Take a separate large bowl, place flour in it, and then stir in remaining ingredients until mixed.

4. Add egg mixture into the bread bucket, top with flour mixture, shut the lid, select the "basic/white" cycle or "low-carb" setting and then press the up/down arrow button to adjust baking time according to your bread machine; it will take 3 to 4 hours.

5.   Then press the crust button to select light crust if available, and press the "start/stop" button to switch on the bread machine.

6.   When the bread machine beeps, open the lid, then take out the bread basket and lift out the bread.

7.   Let bread cool on a wire rack for 1 hour, then cut it into ten slices and serve.

Sesame and Flax Seed Bread

Preparation time: 10 minutes

Cooking time: 4 hours

Total time: 4 hours and 10 minutes

Serving: 1 ½ pounds / 10 slices

Nutritional Info (Per Slice):

230 Cal | 21 g Fat | 6.3 g Protein | 8.2 g Carb | 2 g Fiber | 6.2 g Net Carb

Ingredients:

3 eggs, pasteurized

½ cup / 100 grams cream cheese, softened

6 ½ tablespoons heavy whipping cream

¼ cup / 60 ml melted coconut oil

½ cup / 50 grams almond flour

¼ cup /35 grams flaxseed

6 ½ tablespoons coconut flour

2 2/3 tablespoons sesame seeds

½ teaspoon salt

1½ teaspoon baking powder

2 tablespoons ground psyllium husk powder

½ teaspoon ground caraway seeds

Directions:

1.　Gather all the ingredients for the bread and plug in the bread machine having the capacity of 2 pounds of bread recipe.

2.　Take a large bowl, crack eggs in it and then beat in cream cheese, whipping cream, and coconut oil until well blended.

3.　Take a separate large bowl, place flours in it, and then stir in remaining ingredients until mixed.

4.　Add egg mixture into the bread bucket, top with flour mixture, shut the lid, select the "basic/white" cycle or "low-carb" setting and then press the up/down arrow button to adjust baking time according to your bread machine; it will take 3 to 4 hours.

5.   Then press the crust button to select light crust if available, and press the "start/stop" button to switch on the bread machine.

6.   When the bread machine beeps, open the lid, then take out the bread basket and lift out the bread.

7.   Let bread cool on a wire rack for 1 hour, then cut it into ten slices and serve.

3-Seed Bread

Preparation time: 10 minutes

Cooking time: 4 hours

Total time: 4 hours and 10 minutes

Serving: 2 pounds / 18 slices

Nutritional Info (Per Slice):

139 Cal | 10 g Fat | 5 g Protein | 5.6 g Carb | 3.6 g Fiber | 2 g Net Carb

Ingredients:

2 eggs, pasteurized

¼ cup / 50 grams butter melted

1 cup / 250 ml water warm, at 100°F / 38°C

¼ cup / 35 grams chia seeds

½ cup / 75 grams pumpkin seeds

½ cup / 75 grams psyllium husks

½ cup / 75 grams sunflower seeds

¼ cup / 25 grams coconut flour

1/4 teaspoon salt

1 teaspoon baking powder

Directions:

1.   Gather all the ingredients for the bread and plug in the bread machine having the capacity of 2 pounds of bread recipe.

2.   Take a medium bowl, crack eggs in it and then beat in the butter until well blended.

3.   Take a separate large bowl, place flour in it, and then stir in remaining ingredients except for water until mixed.

4.   Pour water into the bread bucket, add egg mixture, top with flour mixture, shut the lid, select the "basic/white" cycle or "low-carb" setting and then press the up/down arrow button to adjust baking time according to your bread machine; it will take 3 to 4 hours.

5.   Then press the crust button to select light crust if available, and press the "start/stop" button to switch on the bread machine.

6.   When the bread machine beeps, open the lid, then take out the bread basket and lift out the bread.

7.   Let bread cool on a wire rack for 1 hour, then cut it into eighteen slices and serve.

Bacon and Cheddar Bread

Preparation time: 10 minutes

Cooking time: 4 hours

Total time: 4 hours and 10 minutes

Serving: 1 ½ pounds / 9 slices

Nutritional Info (Per Slice):

140 Cal | 12 g Fat | 5 g Protein | 3 g Carb | 1 g Fiber | 2 g Net Carb

Ingredients:

2 eggs, pasteurized

¼ cup / 60 ml beer

2 tablespoons butter, grass-fed, unsalted, melted

¼ cup / 50 grams bacon, pasteurized, cooked, crumbled

½ cup / 120 grams shredded cheddar cheese

½ tablespoon coconut flour

1 cup / 100 grams almond flour

¼ teaspoon salt

½ tablespoon baking powder

Directions:

1.   Gather all the ingredients for the bread and plug in the bread machine having the capacity of 2 pounds of bread recipe.

2.   Take a large bowl, crack eggs in it, beat in beer and butter until blended, and then fold in bacon and cheese until just mixed.

3.   Take a separate large bowl, place flours in it, and then stir in salt and baking powder until mixed.

4.   Add egg mixture into the bread bucket, top with flour mixture, shut the lid, select the "basic/white" cycle or "low-carb" setting and then press the up/down arrow button to adjust baking time according to your bread machine; it will take 3 to 4 hours.

5.   Then press the crust button to select light crust if available, and press the "start/stop" button to switch on the bread machine.

6.   When the bread machine beeps, open the lid, then take out the bread basket and lift out the bread.

7.   Let bread cool on a wire rack for 1 hour, then cut it into nine slices and serve.

Olive Bread

Preparation time: 10 minutes

Cooking time: 4 hours

Total time: 4 hours and 10 minutes

Serving: 1 ½ pounds / 10 slices

Nutritional Info (Per Slice):

85 Cal | 6.5 g Fat | 2 g Protein | 3.4 g Carb | 2.4 g Fiber | 1 g Net Carb

Ingredients:

4 eggs, pasteurized

4 tablespoons avocado oil

1 tablespoon apple cider vinegar

½ cup / 65 grams coconut flour

1 tablespoon baking powder

2 tablespoons psyllium husk powder

1 ½ tablespoons dried rosemary

1/2 teaspoon salt

1/3 cup / 75 grams black olives, chopped

½ cup / 120 ml boiling water

Directions:

1. Gather all the ingredients for the bread and plug in the bread machine having the capacity of 2 pounds of bread recipe.

2. Take a medium bowl, crack eggs in it, blend in oil until combined, stir in vinegar and fold in olives until mixed.

3. Take a separate medium bowl, place flour in it, and then stir in husk powder, baking powder, salt, and rosemary until mixed.

4.   Add egg mixture into the bread bucket, top with flour mixture, shut the lid, select the "basic/white" cycle or "low-carb" setting and then press the up/down arrow button to adjust baking time according to your bread machine; it will take 3 to 4 hours.

5.   Then press the crust button to select light crust if available, and press the "start/stop" button to switch on the bread machine.

6.   When the bread machine beeps, open the lid, then take out the bread basket and lift out the bread.

7.   Let bread cool on a wire rack for 1 hour, then cut it into ten slices and serve.

Jalapeno Cheese Bread

Preparation time: 10 minutes

Cooking time: 4 hours

Total time: 4 hours and 10 minutes

Serving: 1 pound / 8 slices

Nutritional Info (Per Slice):

105 Cal | 6.2 g Fat | 6.6 g Protein | 3.4 g Carb | 1.7 g Fiber | 1.7 g Net Carb

Ingredients:

2 tablespoons Greek yogurt, full-fat

4 eggs, pasteurized

1/3 cup / 40 grams coconut flour

½ teaspoon of sea salt

2 tablespoons whole psyllium husks

1 teaspoon baking powder

¼ cup / 30 grams diced pickled jalapeños

¼ cup / 30 grams shredded cheddar cheese, divided

Directions:

1.   Gather all the ingredients for the bread and plug in the bread machine having the capacity of 1 pound of bread recipe.

2.   Take a large bowl, add yogurt and eggs in it and then beat until well combined.

3.   Take a separate bowl, place flour in it, add remaining ingredients, and stir until mixed.

4.   Add egg mixture into the bread bucket, top with flour mixture, shut the lid, select the "basic/white" cycle or "low-carb" setting and then press the up/down arrow button to adjust baking time according to your bread machine; it will take 3 to 4 hours.

5.   Then press the crust button to select light crust if available, and press the "start/stop" button to switch on the bread machine.

6.   When the bread machine beeps, open the lid, then take out the bread basket and lift out the bread.

7.   Let bread cool on a wire rack for 1 hour, then cut it into eight slices and serve.

Dill and Cheddar Bread

Preparation time: 10 minutes

Cooking time: 4 hours

Total time: 4 hours and 10 minutes

Serving: 2 pounds / 10 slices

Nutritional Info (Per Slice):

292 Cal | 25.2 g Fat | 14.3 g Protein | 6.1 g Carb | 2.6 g Fiber | 3.5 g Net Carb

Ingredients:

4 eggs, pasteurized

¼ teaspoon cream of tartar

5 tablespoons butter, grass-fed, unsalted

2 cups / 470 grams grated cheddar cheese,

1 ½ cups / 150 grams almond flour

1 scoop of egg white protein

1/4 teaspoon salt

1 teaspoon garlic powder

4 teaspoons baking powder

1/4 tablespoon dried dill weed

Directions:

1.   Gather all the ingredients for the bread and plug in the bread machine having the capacity of 2 pounds of bread recipe.

2.   Take a large bowl, crack eggs in it, beat until blended and then beat in cream of tartar, butter, and cheese until just mixed.

3.   Take a separate large bowl, place flour in it, and then stir in egg white protein, salt, garlic powder, baking powder, and dill until mixed.

4.   Add egg mixture into the bread bucket, top with flour mixture, shut the lid, select the "basic/white" cycle or "low-carb" setting and then press the up/down arrow button to adjust baking time according to your bread machine; it will take 3 to 4 hours.

5.   Then press the crust button to select light crust if available, and press the "start/stop" button to switch on the bread machine.

6.   When the bread machine beeps, open the lid, then take out the bread basket and lift out the bread.

7.   Let bread cool on a wire rack for 1 hour, then cut it into ten slices and serve.

Italian Mozzarella and Cream Cheese Bread

Preparation time: 10 minutes

Cooking time: 4 hours

Total time: 4 hours and 10 minutes

Serving: 1 pound / 8 slices

Nutritional Info (Per Slice):

171 Cal | 14.5 g Fat | 3.3 g Protein | 1.5 g Carb | 0.3 g Fiber | 1.2 g Net Carb

Ingredients:

¾ cup / 85 grams shredded mozzarella cheese

¼ cup / 55 grams cream cheese, softened

1 egg, pasteurized

1/3 cup / 35 grams almond flour

¼ teaspoon garlic powder

2 teaspoons baking powder

½ teaspoon Italian seasoning

½ cup / 50 grams shredded cheddar cheese

Directions:

1.   Gather all the ingredients for the bread and plug in the bread machine having the capacity of 1 pound of bread recipe.

2.   Take a medium heatproof bowl, place mozzarella cheese, and cream cheese in it and then microwave for 1 minute until cheese has melted, stirring every 20 seconds.

3.   Meanwhile, take a separate medium bowl, crack the egg in it and beat until blended.

4.   Take a large bowl, place flour in it, add remaining ingredients in it, and stir until mixed.

5.   Add blended egg into the bread bucket, top with melted cheese mixture and then with flour mixture, shut the lid, select the "basic/white" cycle or "low-carb" setting and then press the

up/down arrow button to adjust baking time according to your bread machine; it will take 3 to 4 hours.

6.   Then press the crust button to select light crust if available, and press the "start/stop" button to switch on the bread machine.

7.   When the bread machine beeps, open the lid, then take out the bread basket and lift out the bread.

8.   Let bread cool on a wire rack for 1 hour, then cut it into eight slices and serve.

Sourdough Bread

Preparation time: 10 minutes

Cooking time: 4 hours

Total time: 4 hours and 10 minutes

Serving: 1 ½ pounds / 15 slices

Nutritional Info (Per Slice):

115 Cal | 8 g Fat | 5 g Protein | 4.7 g Carb | 3.6 g Fiber | 1.1 g Net Carb

Ingredients:

2 eggs, pasteurized

6 egg whites, pasteurized

¾ cup / 175 ml coconut milk, unsweetened

¼ cup / 60 ml apple cider vinegar

½ cup / 120 ml warm water, at 100°F / 38°C

1 1/2 cups / 150 grams almond flour

1/2 cup / 65 grams coconut flour

1/2 cup / 65 grams ground flaxseed

1 teaspoon salt

1 teaspoon baking soda

1/3 cup / 65 grams psyllium powder

Directions:

1.   Gather all the ingredients for the bread and plug in the bread machine having the capacity of 2 pounds of bread recipe.

2.   Take a large bowl, add eggs and egg whites in it, pour in milk, add vinegar and water and whisk until combined.

3.   Take a separate large bowl, place flours in it, and then stir in remaining ingredients until mixed.

4.   Add egg mixture into the bread bucket, top with flour mixture, shut the lid, select the "basic/white" cycle or "low-carb" setting and then press the up/down arrow button to adjust baking time according to your bread machine; it will take 3 to 4 hours.

5. Then press the crust button to select light crust if available, and press the "start/stop" button to switch on the bread machine.

6. When the bread machine beeps, open the lid, then take out the bread basket and lift out the bread.

7. Let bread cool on a wire rack for 1 hour, then cut it into fifteen slices and serve.

Cheddar and Herb Bread

Preparation time: 10 minutes

Cooking time: 4 hours

Total time: 4 hours and 10 minutes

Serving: 2 pounds / 16 slices

Nutritional Info (Per Slice):

207 Cal | 17.5 g Fat | 7.2 g Protein | 5 g Carb | 1 g Fiber | 4 g Net Carb

Ingredients:

6 eggs, pasteurized

½ cup / 115 grams butter, grass-fed, unsalted, softened

2 cups / 200 grams almond flour

1 teaspoon baking powder

1/2 teaspoon xanthan gum

2 tablespoons garlic powder

1/2 teaspoon salt

1 tablespoon parsley flakes

1/2 tablespoon dried oregano

1 1/2 cups / 175 grams shredded cheddar cheese

Directions:

1.   Gather all the ingredients for the bread and plug in the bread machine having the capacity of 2 pounds of bread recipe.

2.   Take a large bowl, crack eggs in it, beat until frothy and then beat in the butter until combined.

3.   Take a separate large bowl, place flour in it, and then stir in remaining ingredients until mixed.

4.   Add egg mixture into the bread bucket, top with flour mixture, shut the lid, select the "basic/white" cycle or "low-carb" setting and then press the up/down arrow button to adjust

baking time according to your bread machine; it will take 3 to 4 hours.

5.   Then press the crust button to select light crust if available, and press the "start/stop" button to switch on the bread machine.

6.   When the bread machine beeps, open the lid, then take out the bread basket and lift out the bread.

7.   Let bread cool on a wire rack for 1 hour, then cut it into sixteen slices and serve.

Cumin Bread

Preparation time: 10 minutes

Cooking time: 4 hours

Total time: 4 hours and 10 minutes

Serving: 2 pounds / 12 slices

Nutritional Info (Per Slice):

108 Cal | 8.3 g Fat | 3.7 g Protein | 4 g Carb | 2.8 g Fiber | 1.2 g Net Carb

Ingredients:

2 eggs, pasteurized

1 ½ tablespoons avocado oil

2/3 cup / 150 ml coconut milk, unsweetened

2 tablespoons Picante sauce

1 cup / 100 grams almond flour

½ cup / 65 grams coconut flour

¼ teaspoon salt

1 tablespoon baking powder

¼ teaspoon mustard powder

2 teaspoons ground cumin

Directions:

1.   Gather all the ingredients for the bread and plug in the bread machine having the capacity of 2 pounds of bread recipe.

2.   Take a large bowl, crack eggs in it, beat until frothy and then beat in oil, milk, and Picante sauce until combined.

3.   Take a separate large bowl, place flours in it, and then stir in remaining ingredients until mixed.

4.   Add egg mixture into the bread bucket, top with flour mixture, shut the lid, select the "basic/white" cycle or "low-carb" setting and then press the up/down arrow button to adjust baking time according to your bread machine; it will take 3 to 4 hours.

5.   Then press the crust button to select light crust if available, and press the "start/stop" button to switch on the bread machine.

6. When the bread machine beeps, open the lid, then take out the bread basket and lift out the bread.

7. Let bread cool on a wire rack for 1 hour, then cut it into twelve slices and serve.

Vegetable Loaf

Preparation time: 10 minutes

Cooking time: 4 hours

Total time: 4 hours and 10 minutes

Serving: 2 pounds / 12 slices

Nutritional Info (Per Slice):

181 Cal | 15 g Fat | 6.9 g Protein | 6.6 g Carb | 3 g Fiber | 3.6 g Net
Carb

Ingredients:

4 eggs, pasteurized

1/4 cup / 60 ml coconut oil

1 medium grated zucchini

1 cup / 115 grams grated pumpkin

1 small grated carrot

1/3 cup / 40 grams coconut flour

1 cup / 100 grams almond flour

2 tablespoons pumpkin seeds

2 tablespoons flax seeds

2 tablespoons sunflower seeds

2 tablespoons sesame seeds

2 tablespoons psyllium husks

2 teaspoons salt

1 tablespoon smoked paprika

2 teaspoons ground cumin

2 teaspoons baking powder

Directions:

1. Gather all the ingredients for the bread and plug in the bread machine having the capacity of 1 pound of bread recipe.

2. Take a large bowl, crack eggs in it, beat until frothy, beat in the oil, and then stir in zucchini, pumpkin, and carrot until just mixed.

3. Take a separate large bowl, place flours in it, and then stir in remaining ingredients until mixed.

4. Add egg mixture into the bread bucket, top with flour mixture, shut the lid, select the "basic/white" cycle or "low-carb" setting and then press the up/down arrow button to adjust baking time according to your bread machine; it will take 3 to 4 hours.

5. Then press the crust button to select light crust if available, and press the "start/stop" button to switch on the bread machine.

6. When the bread machine beeps, open the lid, then take out the bread basket and lift out the bread.

7. Let bread cool on a wire rack for 1 hour, then cut it into twelve slices and serve.

Sweet Bread Recipes

Cinnamon Bread

Preparation time: 10 minutes

Cooking time: 4 hours

Total time: 4 hours and 10 minutes

Serving: 2 pounds / 10 slices

Nutritional Info (Per Slice):

169 Cal | 14.5 g Fat | 5.4 g Protein | 4.2 g Carb | 2 g Fiber | 2.2 g Net Carb

Ingredients:

3 tablespoons sour cream

3 eggs, pasteurized

2 teaspoons vanilla extract, unsweetened

¼ cup / 60 grams melted butter, grass-fed, unsalted

2 cups / 200 grams almond flour

1/3 cup / 65 grams erythritol sweetener

2 tablespoons cinnamon

1 teaspoon baking soda

1 teaspoon baking powder

Directions:

1.   Gather all the ingredients for the bread and plug in the bread machine having the capacity of 2 pounds of bread recipe.

2.   Take a large bowl, place sour cream in it and then beat in eggs, vanilla, and butter until combined.

3.   Take a separate large bowl, place flour in it, and then stir in sweetener, cinnamon, baking powder, and soda until mixed.

4.   Add egg mixture into the bread bucket, top with flour mixture, shut the lid, select the "basic/white" cycle setting and then press the up/down arrow button to adjust baking time according to your bread machine; it will take 3 to 4 hours.

5.   Then press the crust button to select light crust if available, and press the "start/stop" button to switch on the bread machine.

6.   When the bread machine beeps, open the lid, then take out the bread basket and lift out the bread.

7.   Let bread cool on a wire rack for 1 hour, then cut it into ten slices and serve.

Banana Bread

Preparation time: 10 minutes

Cooking time: 4 hours

Total time: 4 hours and 10 minutes

Serving: 1 ½ pounds / 12 slices

Nutritional Info (Per Slice):

240 Cal | 21 g Fat | 8.5 g Protein | 6.8 g Carb | 4.2 g Fiber | 2.6 g Net Carb

Ingredients:

2 eggs, pasteurized

1 teaspoon banana extract, unsweetened

¼ cup / 50 grams erythritol sweetener

3 tablespoons butter, grass-fed, unsalted, softened

2 tablespoons almond milk, unsweetened

1 cup / 100 grams almond flour

2 tablespoons coconut flour

¼ cup / 50 grams walnuts, chopped

1 teaspoons baking powder

¼ teaspoon xanthan gum

⅛ teaspoon of sea salt

1 teaspoon cinnamon

Directions:

1.   Gather all the ingredients for the bread and plug in the bread machine having the capacity of 2 pounds of bread recipe.

2.   Take a large bowl, crack eggs in it and then beat in the banana extract, sweetener, butter, and milk until blended.

3.   Take a separate large bowl, place flours in it, and then stir in remaining ingredients until mixed.

4.   Add egg mixture into the bread bucket, top with flour mixture, shut the lid, select the "basic/white" cycle setting and then press the up/down arrow button to adjust baking time according to your bread machine; it will take 3 to 4 hours.

5. Then press the crust button to select light crust if available, and press the "start/stop" button to switch on the bread machine.

6. When the bread machine beeps, open the lid, then take out the bread basket and lift out the bread.

7. Let bread cool on a wire rack for 1 hour, then cut it into twelve slices and serve.

Lemon Raspberry Loaf

Preparation time: 10 minutes

Cooking time: 4 hours

Total time: 4 hours and 10 minutes

Serving: 2 pounds / 12 slices

Nutritional Info (Per Slice):

171 Cal | 14.3 g Fat | 4.6 g Protein | 5 g Carb | 2.4 g Fiber | 2.6 g Net Carb

Ingredients:

2 eggs, pasteurized

4 tablespoons sour cream

1 teaspoon vanilla extract, unsweetened

1 teaspoon lemon extract, unsweetened

4 tablespoons butter, grass-fed, unsalted, melted

1/4 cup / 50 grams erythritol sweetener

2 tablespoons lemon juice

½ cup / 100 grams raspberries preserves

2 cups / 200 grams almond flour

1 ½ teaspoons baking powder

Directions:

1.   Gather all the ingredients for the bread and plug in the bread machine having the capacity of 2 pounds of bread recipe.

2.   Take a large bowl, place flour in it, and then stir in baking soda until mixed.

3.   Take a separate large bowl, crack eggs in it, beat in sour cream, extracts, butter, sweetener, and lemon juice until blended and then stir in raspberry preserve until just combined.

4.   Add egg mixture into the bread bucket, top with flour mixture, shut the lid, select the "basic/white" cycle setting and then press the up/down arrow button to adjust baking time according to your bread machine; it will take 3 to 4 hours.

5.   Then press the crust button to select light crust if available, and press the "start/stop" button to switch on the bread machine.

6.   When the bread machine beeps, open the lid, then take out the bread basket and lift out the bread.

7.   Let bread cool on a wire rack for 1 hour, then cut it into twelve slices and serve.

Walnut Bread

Preparation time: 10 minutes

Cooking time: 4 hours

Total time: 4 hours and 10 minutes

Serving: 1 ½ pounds / 10 slices

Nutritional Info (Per Slice):

201 Cal | 8.1 g Fat | 6 g Protein | 7.5 g Carb | 4.7 g Fiber | 2.8 g Net Carb

Ingredients:

4 eggs, pasteurized

2 tablespoons apple cider vinegar

4 tablespoons coconut oil

1/2 cup / 120 ml lukewarm water

1 cup / 200 grams walnuts chopped

½ cup / 65 grams coconut flour

1 tablespoon baking powder

2 tablespoons psyllium husk powder

1/2 teaspoon salt

Directions:

1.   Gather all the ingredients for the bread and plug in the bread machine having the capacity of 2 pounds of bread recipe.

2.   Take a large bowl, crack eggs in it, beat in vinegar, oil, and water until blended and stir in walnuts until just mixed.

3.   Take a separate large bowl, place flour in it, and then stir in baking powder, husk powder, and salt until mixed.

4.   Add egg mixture into the bread bucket, top with flour mixture, shut the lid, select the "basic/white" cycle setting and then press the up/down arrow button to adjust baking time according to your bread machine; it will take 3 to 4 hours.

5. Then press the crust button to select light crust if available, and press the "start/stop" button to switch on the bread machine.

6. When the bread machine beeps, open the lid, then take out the bread basket and lift out the bread.

7. Let bread cool on a wire rack for 1 hour, then cut it into ten slices and serve.

Almond Butter Bread

Preparation time: 10 minutes

Cooking time: 4 hours

Total time: 4 hours and 10 minutes

Serving: 1 pound / 12 slices

Nutritional Info (Per Slice):

152 Cal | 13 g Fat | 6.4 g Protein | 5.6 g Carb | 3.1 g Fiber | 2.5 g Net Carb

Ingredients:

3 eggs, pasteurized

1 cup / 225 grams almond butter

1 tablespoon apple cider vinegar

1/2 teaspoon baking soda

Directions:

1.   Gather all the ingredients for the bread and plug in the bread machine having the capacity of 1 pound of bread recipe.

2.   Crack eggs in a bowl and then beat in butter, vinegar, and baking soda until combined.

3.   Add egg mixture into the bread bucket, shut the lid, select the "basic/white" cycle setting and then press the up/down arrow button to adjust baking time according to your bread machine; it will take 3 to 4 hours.

4.   Then press the crust button to select light crust if available, and press the "start/stop" button to switch on the bread machine.

5.   When the bread machine beeps, open the lid, then take out the bread basket and lift out the bread.

6.   Let bread cool on a wire rack for 1 hour, then cut it into twelve slices and serve.

Chocolate Zucchini Bread

Preparation time: 10 minutes

Cooking time: 4 hours

Total time: 4 hours and 10 minutes

Serving: 2 pounds / 14 slices

Nutritional Info (Per Slice):

187 Cal | 15.9 g Fat | 6.2 g Protein | 8.8 g Carb | 5.2 g Fiber | 3.6 g Net Carb

Ingredients:

1 cup / 200 grams grated zucchini, moisture squeezed thoroughly

1/3 cup / 60 grams ground flaxseed

½ cup / 100 grams almond flour

1/2 teaspoon salt

2 ½ teaspoons baking powder

1 ¼ tablespoon psyllium husk powder

1/3 cup / 60 grams of cocoa powder

4 eggs, pasteurized

1 tablespoon coconut cream

5 tablespoons coconut oil

¾ cup / 150 grams erythritol sweetener

1 teaspoon vanilla extract, unsweetened

½ cup / 115 grams sour cream

½ cup / 100 grams chocolate chips, unsweetened

Directions:

1.   Wrap zucchini in cheesecloth and twist well until all the moisture is released, set aside until required.

2.   Gather all the ingredients for the bread and plug in the bread machine having the capacity of 2 pounds of bread recipe.

3.   Take a large bowl, place flaxseed and flour in it, and then stir salt, baking powder, husk, and cocoa powder in it until mixed.

4.   Take a separate large bowl, crack eggs in it and then beat in coconut cream, coconut oil, sweetener, and vanilla until combined.

5.　　Blend in half of the flour mixture, then sour cream and remaining half of flour mixture until incorporated and then fold in chocolate chips until mixed.

6.　　Add batter into the bread bucket, shut the lid, select the "basic/white" cycle setting and then press the up/down arrow button to adjust baking time according to your bread machine; it will take 3 to 4 hours.

7.　　Then press the crust button to select light crust if available, and press the "start/stop" button to switch on the bread machine.

8.　　When the bread machine beeps, open the lid, then take out the bread basket and lift out the bread.

9.　　Let bread cool on a wire rack for 1 hour, then cut it into fourteen slices and serve.

Pumpkin Bread

Preparation time: 10 minutes

Cooking time: 4 hours

Total time: 4 hours and 10 minutes

Serving: 1 ½ pound / 12 slices

Nutritional Info (Per Slice):

150 Cal | 12.9 g Fat | 6.7 g Protein | 7 g Carb | 2 g Fiber | 5 g Net Carb

Ingredients:

2 eggs, pasteurized

1 cup / 225 grams almond butter, unsweetened

2/3 cup / 130 grams erythritol sweetener

2/3 cup / 150 grams pumpkin puree

1/8 teaspoon ground cloves

1/2 teaspoon ground cinnamon

1/8 teaspoon ground ginger

1 teaspoon baking powder

1/2 teaspoon ground nutmeg

Directions:

1.   Gather all the ingredients for the bread and plug in the bread machine having the capacity of 2 pounds of bread recipe.

2.   Take a large bowl, crack eggs in it and then beat in remaining ingredients in it in the order described in the ingredients until incorporated.

3.   Add batter into the bread bucket, shut the lid, select the "basic/white" cycle setting and then press the up/down arrow button to adjust baking time according to your bread machine; it will take 3 to 4 hours.

4.   Then press the crust button to select light crust if available, and press the "start/stop" button to switch on the bread machine.

5.   When the bread machine beeps, open the lid, then take out the bread basket and lift out the bread.

6.   Let bread cool on a wire rack for 1 hour, then cut it into twelve slices and serve.

Strawberry Bread

Preparation time: 10 minutes

Cooking time: 4 hours

Total time: 4 hours and 10 minutes

Serving: 2 pounds / 10 slices

Nutritional Info (Per Slice):

201 Cal | 16.4 g Fat | 4.7 g Protein | 6.1 g Carb | 3 g Fiber | 3.1 g
Net Carb

Ingredients:

5 eggs, pasteurized

1 egg white, pasteurized

1 1/2 teaspoons vanilla extract, unsweetened

2 tablespoons heavy whipping cream

2 tablespoons sour cream

1 cup monk fruit powder

1 1/2 teaspoons baking powder

1/2 teaspoon salt

1/2 teaspoon cinnamon

8 tablespoons butter, melted

¾ cup / 100 grams coconut flour

¾ cup / 150 grams chopped strawberries

Directions:

1.   Gather all the ingredients for the bread and plug in the bread machine having the capacity of 2 pounds of bread recipe.

2.   Take a large bowl, crack eggs in it and then beat in egg white, vanilla, heavy cream, sour cream, baking powder, salt, and cinnamon until well combined.

3.   Then stir in coconut flour and fold in strawberries until mixed.

4.   Add batter into the bread bucket, shut the lid, select the "basic/white" cycle or "low-carb" setting and then press the up/down arrow button to adjust baking time according to your bread machine; it will take 3 to 4 hours.

5.   Then press the crust button to select light crust if available, and press the "start/stop" button to switch on the bread machine.

6.   When the bread machine beeps, open the lid, then take out the bread basket and lift out the bread.

7.   Let bread cool on a wire rack for 1 hour, then cut it into ten slices and serve.

Cranberry and Orange Bread

Preparation time: 10 minutes

Cooking time: 4 hours

Total time: 4 hours and 10 minutes

Serving: 1 ½ pound / 12 slices

Nutritional Info (Per Slice):

149 Cal | 13.1 g Fat | 3.9 g Protein | 4 g Carb | 1.5 g Fiber | 2.5 g Net Carb

Ingredients:

1 cup / 200 grams chopped cranberries

2/3 cup and 3 tablespoons / 175 grams monk fruit powder, divided

5 eggs, pasteurized

1 egg white, pasteurized

2 tablespoons sour cream

1 1/2 teaspoons orange extract, unsweetened

1 teaspoon vanilla extract, unsweetened

9 tablespoons butter, grass-fed, unsalted, melted

9 tablespoons coconut flour

1 1/2 teaspoons baking powder

1/4 teaspoon salt

Directions:

1.   Take a small bowl, place cranberries in it, and then stir in 4 tablespoons of monk fruit powder until combined, set aside until required.

2.   Gather all the ingredients for the bread and plug in the bread machine having the capacity of 2 pounds of bread recipe.

3.   Take a large bowl, crack eggs in it, beat in remaining ingredients in it in the order described in the ingredients until incorporated and then fold in cranberries until just mixed.

4.   Add batter into the bread bucket, shut the lid, select the "basic/white" cycle or "low-carb" setting and then press the up/down arrow button to adjust baking time according to your bread machine; it will take 3 to 4 hours.

5.   Then press the crust button to select light crust if available, and press the "start/stop" button to switch on the bread machine.

6.   When the bread machine beeps, open the lid, then take out the bread basket and lift out the bread.

7.   Let bread cool on a wire rack for 1 hour, then cut it into twelve slices and serve.

Blueberry Bread

Preparation time: 10 minutes

Cooking time: 4 hours

Total time: 4 hours and 10 minutes

Serving: 2 pounds

Nutritional Info (Per Slice):

211 Cal | 18.2 g Fat | 7.7 g Protein | 8.9 g Carb | 3.7 g Fiber | 5.2 g Net Carb

Ingredients:

4 eggs, pasteurized

3 tablespoons heavy whipping cream

3 tablespoons butter, grass-fed, unsalted, melted

1 teaspoon vanilla extract, unsweetened

2 tablespoons coconut flour

2 cups / 200 grams almond flour

1/2 cup / 100 grams erythritol sweetener

1 1/2 teaspoons baking powder

1 cup / 200 grams blueberries

Directions:

1.   Gather all the ingredients for the bread and plug in the bread machine having the capacity of 2 pounds of bread recipe.

2.   Take a large bowl, crack eggs in it and then beat in cream, butter, and vanilla until combined.

3.   Take a separate large bowl, place flours in it, then stir in sweetener and baking powder until mixed and fold in blueberries.

4.   Add egg mixture into the bread bucket, top with flour mixture, shut the lid, select the "basic/white" cycle or "low-carb" setting and then press the up/down arrow button to adjust

baking time according to your bread machine; it will take 3 to 4 hours.

5.   Then press the crust button to select light crust if available, and press the "start/stop" button to switch on the bread machine.

6.   When the bread machine beeps, open the lid, then take out the bread basket and lift out the bread.

7.   Let bread cool on a wire rack for 1 hour, then cut it into eleven slices and serve.

Chocolate Bread

Preparation time: 10 minutes

Cooking time: 4 hours

Total time: 4 hours and 10 minutes

Serving: 1 ½ pounds / 8 slices

Nutritional Info (Per Slice):

214 Cal | 18 g Fat | 6.4 g Protein | 6.6 g Carb | 2.9 g Fiber | 3.7 g Net Carb

Ingredients:

3 eggs, pasteurized

¼ cup / 50 grams swerve sweetener

¼ cup / 60 ml melted coconut oil

2 tablespoons almond flour

¼ cup / 35 grams coconut flour

¼ tablespoon salt

2 tablespoons whey protein powder

½ teaspoon baking soda

½ cup / 75 grams of cocoa powder

2 tablespoons mini chocolate chips, sugar-free

Directions:

1.   Gather all the ingredients for the bread and plug in the bread machine having the capacity of 2 pounds of bread recipe.

2.   Take a large bowl, crack eggs in it, beat until frothy and then beat in swerve sweetener and oil until fluffy.

3.   Take a separate large bowl, place flours in it, and then stir in remaining ingredients until mixed.

4.   Add egg mixture into the bread bucket, top with flour mixture, shut the lid, select the "basic/white" cycle or "low-carb" setting and then press the up/down arrow button to adjust baking time according to your bread machine; it will take 3 to 4 hours.

5.   Then press the crust button to select light crust if available, and press the "start/stop" button to switch on the bread machine.

6. When the bread machine beeps, open the lid, then take out the bread basket and lift out the bread.

7. Let bread cool on a wire rack for 1 hour, then cut it into eight slices and serve.

Sweet Avocado Bread

Preparation time: 10 minutes

Cooking time: 4 hours

Total time: 4 hours and 10 minutes

Serving: 1 ½ pounds / 12 slices

Nutritional Info (Per Slice):

94 Cal | 6.1 g Fat | 4.2 g Protein | 3.2 g Carb | 2.7 g Fiber | 0.5 g Net Carb

Ingredients:

3 eggs, pasteurized

2 tablespoons erythritol sweetener

1 tablespoon vanilla extract, unsweetened

1 ½ cups / 300 grams mashed avocado mashed, ripe

6 tablespoons coconut flour

3/4 teaspoon baking soda

1/2 teaspoon salt

2 tablespoons cocoa powder, unsweetened

Directions:

1.   Gather all the ingredients for the bread and plug in the bread machine having the capacity of 2 pounds of bread recipe.

2.   Take a large bowl, crack eggs in it, beat in sweetener and vanilla until fluffy and then mix in avocado.

3.   Take a separate large bowl, place flour in it, and then stir in remaining ingredients until mixed.

4.   Add egg mixture into the bread bucket, top with flour mixture, shut the lid, select the "basic/white" cycle or "low-carb" setting and then press the up/down arrow button to adjust baking time according to your bread machine; it will take 3 to 4 hours.

5.　Then press the crust button to select light crust if available, and press the "start/stop" button to switch on the bread machine.

6.　When the bread machine beeps, open the lid, then take out the bread basket and lift out the bread.

7.　Let bread cool on a wire rack for 1 hour, then cut it into twelve slices and serve.

Thanks for buying *Keto Bread Machine Recipes!*

If you found the recipes amazing and delicious, please share your thoughts, successes and failures on the book's Amazon.com reviews.

About The Author

Marie Folher grew up in Strasbourg, France and she fell in love with baking as a kid. She moved to California at the age of 21 and she found a job from a small bakery. Since then, she has baked countless amounts of different baked goods. She has had time to experiment with many different flavor combinations, and with trial and error, she has found, and still finds, amazing recipes

She loves experimenting with different diets because it opens new worlds of different kinds of baked goods and food for her. At the moment, in 2020, she's following keto diet since she has found it the king of all diets in maintaining a healthy body. She's had time to try new recipes and she's been awed of how good food the keto-friendly food can be. With her cookbooks, she wants to share her best recipes with you.

Books by Marie Folher

Bundt Cake Recipes – 30
Delicious Bundt Cake Recipes
From Scratch

Keto Chaffle Recipes – 30
Easy Fast and Super Delicious
Ketogenic Chaffle Recipes

Keto Bread Machine Recipes
– 30 Easy, Healthy and Low-
Carb Ketogenic Bread
Machine Recipes

Keto Bread Recipes – 30
Easy, Healthy and Super
Delicious Low-Carb
Ketogenic Bread Recipes

Artisan Bread Recipes –
Artisan Bread Cookbook Full
of Easy, Simple And
Mouthwatering Artisan Bread
Recipes

Bread Machine Cookbook –
Simple and Easy-To-Follow
Bread Machine Recipes for
Mouthwatering Homemade
Bread

Image Credits

Cover image: Designed by Freepik

Yeast Bread: iStock.com/Oxana Medvedeva

Cream Cheese Bread: iStock.com/PaulPaladin

Lemon Poppy Seed Bread: iStock.com/rclassenlayouts

Almond Meal Bread: iStock.com/apomares

Macadamia Nut Bread: iStock.com/Mariha-kitchen

Cauliflower and Garlic Bread: iStock.com/radu984

Cheesy Garlic Bread: iStock.com/Sezeryadigar

Rosemary Bread: iStock.com/Mizina

Sesame and Flax Seed Bread: iStock.com/kajakiki

3-Seed Bread: iStock.com/Ilse Bermúdez

Bacon and Cheddar Bread: iStock.com/Zakharova_Natalia

Olive Bread: iStock.com/ballycroy

Jalapeno Cheese Bread: iStock.com/fotogal

Dill and Cheddar Bread: iStock.com/schmez

Italian Mozzarella and Cream Cheese Bread: iStock.com/Eivaisla

Sourdough Bread: iStock.com/fcafotodigital

Cheddar and Herb Bread: iStock.com/baibaz

Cumin Bread: iStock.com/jonathan_steven

Vegetable Loaf: iStock.com/NightAndDayImages

Cinnamon Bread: iStock.com/margouillatphotos

Banana Bread: iStock.com/cujo19

Lemon Raspberry Loaf: iStock.com/manyakotic

Walnut Bread: iStock.com/asab974

Almond Butter Bread: iStock.com/EasterBunnyUK

Chocolate Zucchini Bread: iStock.com/DreamBigPhotos

Pumpkin Bread: iStock.com/tvirbickis

Strawberry Bread: iStock.com/Jmichl

Cranberry and Orange Bread: iStock.com/iko636

Blueberry Bread: iStock.com/stphillips

Chocolate Bread: iStock.com/Lena_Zajchikova

Sweet Avocado Bread: iStock.com/rudisill